National Security Agency/Central Security Service

Information

Assurance

Directorate

Deploying and Securing Google Chrome in a Windows Enterprise

October 22, 2012
Revision 1

A product of the Network Components and Applications Division

ADF-2012-1216

Contents

1   Introduction 1

2   Deployment 2

     2.1   Version Management 2

     2.2   Import Policy Templates 3

     2.3   Initial Deployment 4

     2.4   Update Deployment 5

     2.5   Policy Updates 6

3   Policies 6

     3.1   User Settings and User Cache Location 8

     3.2   Default Search Provider 9

     3.3   Safe Browsing 9

     3.4   Protocol Schemes 10

     3.5   3D Graphics 10

     3.6   Cookies 10

     3.7   JavaScript 11

     3.8   Plugins 12

     3.9   Extensions 15

4   Google Update 18

5   Appendix 20

     5.1   Appendix A: Binaries Installed by Chrome 20

     5.2   Appendix B: Chrome Policy Registry Data 21

         5.2.1   Mapping Policy Names to Registry Data 21

         5.2.2   Example Policy Registry Data 23

     5.3   Appendix C: Chrome Extension Permissions and Warnings 26

     5.4   Appendix D: PowerShell Scripts 31

List of Figures

Figure 1: Chrome Group Policy location 3

Figure 2: Deploying Chrome via Group Policy software installation 4

Figure 3: Chrome Application folder containing the current and previous version of Chrome 5

Figure 4: Using the Omnibox configured with a secure default search provider 9

Figure 5: The blocked cookie notification icon in the Chrome Omnibox 11

Figure 6: Web content for a plugin that has been disabled due to being outdated 14

Figure 7: Example of a high risk extension in the Chrome Web Store 16

Figure 8: Chrome extension installation prompt displaying a permission warning 16

Figure 9: An extension ID in a Chrome Web Store URL 17

Figure 10: Windows scheduled tasks for the Google Update service 18

Figure 11: Windows services for the Google Update service 18

List of Tables

Table 1: Recommended Chrome policies and values 8

Table 2: Chrome variables for Windows and their corresponding file system locations 9

Table 3: Default search provider values for Google encrypted search 9

Table 4: Example policies for allowing cookies on specific web sites 10

Table 5: Example policies for allowing JavaScript to run on specific web sites 12

Table 6: Default plugins installed with Chrome 12

Table 7: Common plugins available for Chrome 13

Table 8: Example URL whitelist allowing plugins to run on specific web sites 14

Table 9: Chrome extension risk categorization based on permissions 15

Table 10: Example Chrome extensions 17

Table 11: Example values for the force install extensions policy 17

Table 12: Binaries for Chrome 20

Table 13: Binaries for Google Update 20

Table 14: Mapping of Chrome Group Policy names to registry key or value names 23

Table 15: Chrome warning messages and their corresponding permission entry 30

Disclaimer

This Guide is provided "as is." Any express or implied warranties, including but not limited to, the implied warranties of merchantability and fitness for a particular purpose are disclaimed. In no event shall the United States Government be liable for any direct, indirect, incidental, special, exemplary or consequential damages (including, but not limited to, procurement of substitute goods or services, loss of use, data or profits, or business interruption) however caused and on any theory of liability, whether in contract, strict liability, or tort (including negligence or otherwise) arising in any way out of the use of this Guide, even if advised of the possibility of such damage.

The User of this Guide agrees to hold harmless and indemnify the United States Government, its agents and employees from every claim or liability (whether in tort or in contract), including attorneys' fees, court costs, and expenses, arising in direct consequence of Recipient's use of the item, including, but not limited to, claims or liabilities made for injury to or death of personnel of User or third parties, damage to or destruction of property of User or third parties, and infringement or other violations of intellectual property or technical data rights.

Nothing in this Guide is intended to constitute an endorsement, explicit or implied, by the U.S. Government of any particular manufacturer's product or service.

Trademark Information

This publication has not been authorized, sponsored, or otherwise approved by Google Inc.

Chrome™, Chromium™, Google™, Google Chrome™, Google Chrome Extensions™, Google Code™, Google Instant™, Google Safe Browsing™, Google Suggest™, Google Sync™, Google Translate, ™ and Google Updater™ are trademarks of Google Inc.

Microsoft®, Windows®, Silverlight®, Office®, Windows Vista®, Active Directory®, and Windows PowerShell® are either registered trademarks or trademarks of Microsoft Corporation in the United States and/or other countries.

Adobe Flash®, Adobe Shockwave®, Adobe PDF®, and Adobe Reader® are either registered trademarks or trademarks of Adobe Systems Incorporated in the United States and/or other countries.

Oracle® and Java® are registered trademarks of Oracle and/or its affiliates. Other names may be trademarks of their respective owners.

Apple® and QuickTime® are trademarks of Apple Inc., registered in the U.S. and other countries.

RealPlayer® is a trademark or registered trademark of RealNetworks, Inc.

1 Introduction

Google Chrome is a widely used, free web browser developed by Google based on the open source Chromium project. Chrome has been available for consumers since 2008. Starting in 2010, Google released an enterprise version of Chrome that is configurable through Group Policy and deployable with a Windows Installer (MSI) file. These improvements make Chrome a manageable and deployable browser in Windows domains.

Chrome supports modern security features[1], such as sandboxing and safe browsing, which are designed to help protect users and enterprise networks from malicious web sites. Chrome also supports enhanced web site certificate checking mechanisms and automatic updates.

The Chrome sandbox is a security feature that helps protect users by preventing an exploit from gaining highly privileged access to the system due to a vulnerability in Chrome. The security provided by the sandbox on Windows systems is strongest when running Chrome on Windows Vista or newer operating system versions since the sandbox leverages security mechanisms added to the operating system starting with Windows Vista. Google released Chrome 8 in 2010 with an included Adobe PDF reader plugin that runs inside a protected sandbox. Google released Chrome 21 in 2012 with an included Adobe Flash plugin that runs inside a protected sandbox. These security enhancements limit the damage from common attack vectors.

The Chrome safe browsing feature displays a warning message for web sites that are known to contain malware or phishing attacks by looking up web sites in a known bad list maintained by Google. It is important to note that safe browsing does not send web site URL information to Google. This provides a security benefit without compromising privacy.

In addition to supporting industry standard web site certificate validation mechanisms, Chrome also has a feature called CRLSet[2] that checks web site certificates against a locally stored list of revoked certificates. This feature allows certificate revocation checks to occur even when the Certificate Authority cannot be contacted to verify the revocation status of the certificate. Chrome automatically updates the certificate revocation data without requiring a new version of Chrome to be installed and the updates take effect without having to restart the browser.

Chrome automatically updates using Google Update. The Chrome updates are signed by Google and are retrieved using a secure connection. Chrome also automatically updates some included plugins, any extensions that support automatic updates, and certificate revocation data. Google releases Chrome updates at a quick pace which leads to vulnerabilities being promptly patched.

This paper contains deployment guidance, recommended policies, and technical details for United States government and Department of Defense administrators who want to use the enterprise version of the Google Chrome web browser in their Windows Active Directory domain. Chrome 20.0.1132.47,

---

[1] Chromium Security. http://chromium.org/Home/chromium-security
[2] Revocation checking and Chrome's CRL. http://www.imperialviolet.org/2012/02/05/crlsets.html

20.0.1132.57, and 21.0.1180.60 were tested on Windows 7 for the initial publication of this guide. The guide has been updated to include new policies and remove deprecated policies in Chrome 22 and was tested against Chrome version 22.0.119.79 on Windows 7. Future updates will only happen when new relevant policies are introduced, when old policies are deprecated, or when policy recommendations change.

2 Deployment

An administrator must download the latest version of the Chrome Windows Installer (MSI)[3] file and the corresponding Chrome Group Policy templates[4] before deploying Chrome. Rename the MSI file to include the full version number of Chrome since Google uses the same file name no matter which version of Chrome the MSI file represents. The administrator should place the MSI file at a network path that is accessible to workstations and is readable by domain users.

2.1 Version Management

Deploying and updating Google Chrome may be handled in two ways. The first method is deploying Chrome and leaving automatic updates enabled which is the default behavior. The Google Update service is responsible for keeping Chrome updated to the newest version. This method is recommended since Chrome is updated frequently and these updates often contain critical security fixes. This method is especially beneficial for enterprises where IT staff is either not trained or not available for monitoring, testing, and deploying new versions to keep pace with a frequent release schedule.

The second method is disabling automatic updates and manually deploying new versions of Chrome as they are released. The overhead of manually testing and deploying each version of Chrome that is released, while trying to keep up with frequent releases, may be considerable. This method is more suitable for enterprises that have full time staff dedicated to testing and deploying software updates in a timely fashion. IT staff may find it a better investment in allowing Chrome to automatically update itself so they may focus on testing and deploying software updates for software that is commonly exploited by attackers.

Major Chrome stable channel releases occur about every 6 weeks. Approximately 3-6 minor versions may be released before the next major version. Even minor Chrome stable channel updates are important to install since they frequently contain critical security fixes. Since Chrome is an open source browser, attackers can see the exact code changes made for a security fix which could assist them in attacking outdated versions of Chrome. Running the most recently patched version of Chrome is always recommended to prevent exploitation of known vulnerabilities. Google only officially supports the latest stable channel release of Chrome. The latest stable channel version number for Chrome on Windows can be found at **http://omahaproxy.appspot.com/win**.

---

[3] Chrome Browser for Businesses. http://www.google.com/intl/en/chrome/business/browser
[4] Policy Templates – The Chromium Projects. http://www.chromium.org/administrators/policy-templates

2.2 Import Policy Templates

The Chrome policy_template.zip file contains both ADM and ADMX versions of the Group Policy settings. Enterprises using Windows Server 2008 or above can use the ADM or the ADMX policy file. If using Windows Server 2003 to manage domain policies, then use the ADM file.

Before deploying Chrome, use the Group Policy Management snap-in to create a new Group Policy Object (GPO) for Chrome policies. Apply this newly created GPO to the Organization Unit(s) within the domain for which Chrome will be installed and managed.

If Chrome is installed on servers or workstations used for administrative tasks, then consider using a separate GPO that enforces more strict policies such as Chrome's URL whitelisting policy[5] to only allow access to specific internal web sites. Internet web browsing should never be performed on privileged workstations or servers. Administrators should also enforce more strict policies that limit execution of JavaScript and browser plugins to specific internal web sites on privileged workstations or servers. See the JavaScript and Plugins sections for examples.

The steps below demonstrate how to import the ADM template file into the new GPO using the Group Policy Management Editor.

1. Extract the Chrome policy_template.zip file. The chrome.adm file for the English language can be found in **\policy_templates\windows\adm\en-US\chrome.adm**.
2. Navigate to **Computer Configuration** > **Policies** > **Administrative Templates**. Right click on **Administrative Templates** and select **Add/Remove Templates**.
3. In the Add/Remove Templates dialog, click the **Add** button and select the chrome.adm file from the extracted Chrome policy templates location.
4. Once the template is loaded, Chrome policies can be managed by navigating to **Computer Configuration** > **Policies** > **Administrative Templates** > **Google** > **Google Chrome** and then configuring the appropriate individual policy settings as shown in Figure 1 below.

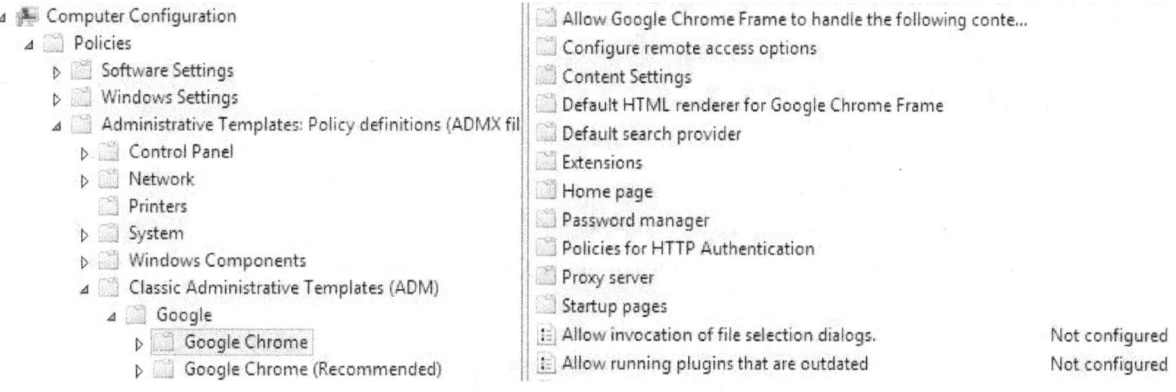

Figure 1: Chrome Group Policy location

---

[5] URL Whitelist. http://www.chromium.org/administrators/policy-list-3#URLWhitelist

Notice in Figure 1 that there are two folders that contain Chrome policies: **Google Chrome** and **Google Chrome (Recommended)**. The policies in the **Google Chrome (Recommended)** folder are a subset of the policies contained in the **Google Chrome** folder. If policies are configured under the **Google Chrome (Recommended)** folder, then these policies are only effective if the same policies are *not* configured under the **Google Chrome** folder. This behavior may not be intuitive to Windows administrators so only configuring policies under the **Google Chrome** folder is recommended to prevent confusion. While the policies under the **Google Chrome (Recommended)** folder can be used to set defaults for user overridable options, a Windows administrator can achieve the same effect by configuring policies under the **Google Chrome** folder within the User Configuration section of Group Policy rather than Computer Configuration section.

2.3 Initial Deployment

Deployment of Google Chrome in a Windows enterprise is straightforward. An administrator should determine which of the three common deployment methods they will use:

1. A commercial software deployment tool.
2. Windows Group Policy software installation.
3. A computer startup or shutdown script.

This paper only covers the Windows Group Policy software installation deployment method since it is available at no extra cost and is easier to use than a script.

Use the Group Policy Object created in the Import Policy Templates section for configuring Chrome policies or use the Group Policy Management snap-in to create a new GPO for Chrome deployment. To deploy Chrome using Windows Group Policy software installation:

1. In the Group Policy Management Editor, navigate to **Computer Configuration** > **Policies** > **Software Settings** > **Software installation**, right click on **Software installation**, and select **New** > **Package**. This will display an Open File dialog.
2. Browse to the network path location of the Chrome MSI file. Make sure the network location of the MSI file is accessible to workstations and that domain users have read access to it. Select the MSI and click the **OK** button. This will open the Deploy Software dialog.
3. In the Deploy Software dialog, leave the default selection and then click the **OK** button and wait a few seconds for the Group Policy Management Editor to show the newly published package as shown in Figure 2 below. It may take some time for the new Group Policy settings to apply to systems and it may also take 2-3 reboots before the package is installed on the system.

Figure 2: Deploying Chrome via Group Policy software installation

The user friendly Chrome version number will not match the version reported in the software installation Group Policy window. Notice in Figure 2 the Version column shows a value of 65.27 for a deployment of Chrome 20.0.1132.47. The same value will display for a deployment of Chrome 20.0.1132.57. Chrome 21.0.1180.60 will display a value of 65.39. Renaming the Chrome MSI file so that it includes the full user friendly Chrome version number information is recommended to prevent confusion about which version of Chrome is being deployed by the software installation policy. Also note that when checking the Chrome version information in the Programs and Features dialog in Windows, the version number will not match the full user friendly Chrome version number either. For example, Chrome 20.0.1132.47 displays as 65.27.47, Chrome 20.0.1132.57 displays as 65.27.57, and Chrome 21.0.1180.60 displays as 65.39.60 in the Programs and Features dialog.

It is possible that users may have already installed the consumer version of Chrome since it does not require administrative privileges to install. Deploying the enterprise version of Chrome will remove an existing consumer installation of Chrome but will retain user settings and preferences.

2.4 Update Deployment

Enterprises that choose to disable the automatic update mechanisms provided by Google Update can use the Group Policy software installation feature to manually deploy new versions of Chrome. To deploy a new version of Chrome using Group Policy software installation:

1. Right click on the currently assigned software installation policy for Chrome, as shown in Figure 2, and select **All Tasks > Remove**.
2. At the Remove Software dialog, select **Allow users to continue to use the software, but prevent new installations** and click the **OK** button. This will leave Chrome installed on systems.
3. Now create a new Group Policy software installation policy for the new version of Chrome, using the same directions listed in the Initial Deployment section, but select the new Chrome MSI file.

The above steps result in the same upgrade behavior that happens with Chrome's automatic update mechanism. The Chrome MSI correctly upgrades over the existing installation using the Group Policy software installation mechanism just like it does when using Chrome automatic updates. Chrome leaves folders from previous versions behind, in case a rollback is needed, as shown in Figure 3.

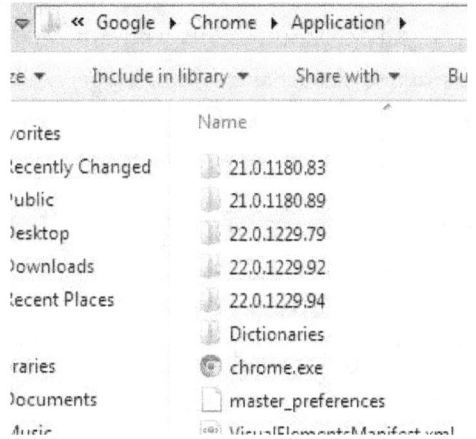

Figure 3: Chrome Application folder containing the current and previous version of Chrome

5

Administrators may want to create maintenance scripts to remove the old folders since each folder uses 100MB to 200MB of disk space. The old versions should only be removed after administrators have verified the new version of Chrome is working correctly.

2.5 Policy Updates

Administrators should download the latest Chrome Group Policy templates when a major version of Chrome is released. Major Chrome releases may have new policies added or current policies removed due to being deprecated. Administrators should compare the policy templates for the current version of Chrome they are using against the newly downloaded policy templates and note any additions or removals. This can be achieved by using a file comparison tool to review the changes between the two versions of the templates.

Administrators can also identify deprecated policies in Chrome by installing the new version of Chrome but not immediately updating the policy templates used in their Chrome GPO to the latest policy templates. Then administrators can check the Chrome policies tab for deprecated policies by opening **chrome://policy** and looking for the text **This policy has been deprecated** under the **Status** column. This notice is displayed since Chrome still recognizes the registry data associated with deprecated policies for approximately 4 major releases of Chrome before it is completely removed.

Before administrators update the Chrome GPO with the latest policy template they should first modify any deprecated policies in their current GPO. Use the Group Policy Management Editor to set all the deprecated policies to **Not Configured**. The registry data for the deprecated policies will be removed from systems once Group Policy updates have been applied. If this procedure isn't used, then registry data for the deprecated policies will remain indefinitely. Once Group Policy updates have been applied to all systems, then administrators should update their Chrome GPO to use the latest Chrome Group Policy template and configure any newly added policies.

3 Policies

Table 1 contains a list of recommended policies and values to harden and secure Chrome. These policies are based on a balance between usability and security and are recommended for most enterprises. Some policies could be further hardened or relaxed based on operational needs of the network and are discussed as optional example policies in the sections within the Policies section. Complete policy descriptions can be found on the Chrome Policy List web page[6].

The policies in this guide are configured within the Computer Configuration section of Group Policy under the **Google Chrome** folder. These policies will create registry keys and values on systems under the registry key of **HKLM\Software\Policies\Google\Chrome**. See Appendix B for a complete mapping of all policy names to their registry values and example registry data that corresponds to the recommended and example optional policies from this guide.

---

[6] Chrome Policy List. http://www.chromium.org/administrators/policy-list-3

A home user can also install the enterprise version of Chrome and import the policy templates into Windows local policy, if they are running a version of Windows which supports local policy, to take advantage of the policies in this guide.

DoD administrators should also consult the Defense Information Systems Agency (DISA) Security Technical Implementation Guide (STIG) for Chrome[7]. The DISA STIG for Chrome provides policies, in addition to the policies in Table 1, and Security Content Automation Protocol (SCAP) data which can be used for automated compliance checking.

Policy Path	Policy Name	Policy State	Policy Value
Google Chrome\Configure remote access options\	Enable firewall traversal from remote access host	Disabled	
Google Chrome\Content Settings\	Default geolocation setting	Enabled	Do not allow any site to track the users' physical location
Google Chrome\Content Settings\	Default mediastream setting	Enabled	Do not allow any site to access my camera and microphone
Google Chrome\Content Settings\	Default notification setting	Enabled	Do not allow any site to show desktop notifications
Google Chrome\Content Settings\	Default popups setting	Enabled	Do not allow any site to show popups
Google Chrome\Extensions\	Configure extension installation blacklist	Enabled	*
Google Chrome\Extensions\	Configure extension installation whitelist	Enabled	*Add the extension IDs for any approved extensions otherwise leave Policy State as Not Configured*
Google Chrome\Password manager	Allow users to show passwords in Password Manager	Disabled	
Google Chrome\Password manager	Enable the password manager	Disabled	
Google Chrome\Policies for HTTP Authentication	Supported authentication	Enabled	negotiate
Google Chrome\	Allow running plugins that are outdated	Disabled	
Google Chrome\	Always runs plugins that require authorization	Disabled	
Google Chrome\	Continue running background apps when Google Chrome is closed	Disabled	
Google Chrome\	Disable proceeding from the Safe Browsing warning page	Enabled	
Google Chrome\	Disable saving browser history	Disabled	
Google Chrome\	Disable SPDY protocol	Enabled	
Google Chrome\	Disable support for 3D graphics APIs	Enabled	
Google Chrome\	Disable synchronization of data with Google	Enabled	
Google Chrome\	Disable taking screenshots	Enabled	
Google Chrome\	Disable URL protocol schemes	Enabled	file, javascript
Google Chrome\	Enable AutoFill	Disabled	
Google Chrome\	Enable Google Cloud Print proxy	Disabled	
Google Chrome\	Enable Instant	Disabled	
Google Chrome\	Enable network prediction	Disabled	
Google Chrome\	Enable reporting of usage and crash-related data	Disabled	

---

[7] Application Security - Browser Guidance. http://iase.disa.mil/stigs/browser_guidance/browser_guidance.html

Policy Path	Policy Name	Policy State	Policy Value
Google Chrome\	Enable Safe Browsing	Enabled	
Google Chrome\	Enable search suggestions	Disabled	
Google Chrome\	Enable submission of documents to Google Cloud Print	Disabled	
Google Chrome\	Import saved passwords from default browser on first run	Disabled	
Google Chrome\	Incognito mode availability	Enabled	Incognito mode disabled
Google Chrome\	Specify a list of disabled plugins	Enabled	*
Google Chrome\	Specify a list of enabled plugins	Enabled	Shockwave Flash, Chrome PDF Viewer
Google Chrome\	Specify whether the plugin finder should be disabled	Enabled	
Google Chrome\	Whether online OCSP/CRL checks are performed	Enabled	

Table 1: Recommended Chrome policies and values

Note that some policies only need to change their state to Enabled or Disabled as shown in the Policy State column. Other policies may need additional configuration which is noted in the Policy Value column. Some of the Policy State and Policy Value combinations may seem unintuitive but they have been tested to ensure they enforce the correct behavior. Some of the policies from Table 1 are discussed in more detail in the following sections of the paper.

3.1 User Settings and User Cache Location

The **Set user data directory** policy is used to determine where user data, such as bookmarks and history, is stored. By default this data is stored in a Chrome user data folder under the path of C:\Users\<user>\AppData\Local\Google\Chrome\User Data\. The data stored under the AppData's Local folder does not roam when Windows roaming profiles are used. Enterprises that use roaming profiles may want to change the previously mentioned Chrome policy so the Chrome user data folder will be stored in the user's roaming profile. For example, setting the policy value to **${roaming_app_data}\Chrome** results in various user data folders and files getting created under the path of C:\Users\<user>\AppData\Roaming\Chrome\. The AppData's Roaming folder roams when Windows roaming profiles are used.

Now that the user data folder is stored in the user's roaming profile, the temporary Chrome cache files will also be stored in the user's roaming profile at C:\Users\<user>\AppData\Roaming\Chrome\User Data\Default\Cache\. Enterprises may want to change the cache storage location so the cache is stored at a location that does not roam. The cache location is controlled by the **Set disk cache directory** policy. Setting the policy value to **${local_app_data}\Chrome** results in a cache folder getting created under the path of C:\Users\<user>\AppData\Local\Chrome\. Table 2 contains a list of some of the Chrome variables[8] that can be used to specify different paths in Windows.

Chrome Variable Name	Windows Path Location
${roaming_app_data}	C:\Users\<user>\AppData\Roaming
${local_app_data}	C:\Users\<user>\AppData\Local
${documents}	C:\Users\<user>\My Documents

---

[8] Supported Directory Variables. http://www.chromium.org/administrators/policy-list-3/user-data-directory-variables

Chrome Variable Name	Windows Path Location
${profile}	C:\Users\<user>
${global_app_data}	C:\Users\All Users\AppData

Table 2: Chrome variables for Windows and their corresponding file system locations

Note that when a Chrome update is installed, the enterprise Chrome installer is not aware of the **Set user data directory** and **Set disk cache directory** policies so the installer will still create folders containing default data at C:\Users\<user>\AppData\Local\Google\. Chrome uses those policy values when it is launched by the user.

3.2 Default Search Provider

Some enterprises may want to have a standard default search provider. Setting a default search provider allows users to perform searches without having to first visit a search engine's web page. If setting a specific default search provider is desired, then using a provider that supports HTTPS connections is recommended. The example in Table 3 shows how to configure the policies under **Google\Google Chrome\Default search provider** to set https://encrypted.google.com as the default search provider.

Policy Name	Policy State	Policy Value
Enable the default search provider	Enabled	
Default search provider name	Enabled	Google Encrypted Search
Default search provider search URL	Enabled	https://encrypted.google.com/search?{google:acceptedSuggestion}{google:originalQueryForSuggestion}sourceid=chrome&ie={inputEncoding}&q={searchTerms}

Table 3: Default search provider values for Google encrypted search

If users type text into the Omnibox that is not a URL, then a secure search will be performed. The Omnibox is the name for Chrome's address bar as shown in Figure 4.

Figure 4: Using the Omnibox configured with a secure default search provider

3.3 Safe Browsing

The Chrome safe browsing feature displays a warning message for web sites that are known to contain malware or phishing attacks by looking up web sites in a list of known bad web sites maintained by Google. It is important to note that safe browsing does not send web site URL information to Google. Instead, a list of known bad web sites is downloaded to the system. This download occurs silently in the background when Chrome is running. As a user browses web sites, the URLs are checked against the locally stored list of bad web sites. This provides a security benefit without compromising privacy. In some cases a SHA1 hash of a URL is sent to Google for further safety verification but even then the clear text URL is not sent in order to protect the user's privacy. Setting the **Enable Safe Browsing** policy to **Enabled** is recommended since this feature can effectively block initial malware infections.

3.4 Protocol Schemes

Chrome supports handling of a number of protocol schemes. Setting the **Disable URL protocol schemes** policy to **Enabled** and setting its value to **file, javascript** is recommended to block arbitrary file system access and to block arbitrary execution of JavaScript in the Omnibox.

Administrators can add more protocol schemes as necessary based on their network's operational security needs. For example, **ftp** could be added to the policy to block Chrome from handling File Transfer Protocol (FTP) connections. A value of **view-source** could be added to the policy to prevent users from viewing the source of web pages.

3.5 3D Graphics

By default Chrome supports WebGL which is a technology that renders 3D graphics in a web browser using hardware acceleration from the Graphics Processing Unit (GPU) of modern video cards. Currently, there are very few web sites that use this technology so disabling it has little effect on users and reduces the attack surface. However, WebGL is sandboxed due to running in the sandboxed Chrome GPU rendering process. Setting the **Disable support for 3D graphics API's** policy to **Enabled**, unless 3D content is required, is recommended. If 3D content is required, then set this policy back to **Not Configured**.

3.6 Cookies

Cookies are often used by web sites to store stateful data in the browser that can be used again the next time a user visits the web site[9]. Chrome has the ability through policy to block cookies from all web sites. This setting may break many web sites that use cookies to manage a user's login or logout state. It is possible to block cookies from all web sites and then selectively whitelist domains or web sites where cookies are allowed[10]. Applying this policy to all user workstations comes with an extremely high administrative overhead for managing the whitelist depending on the level of granularity used. Administrators may also not be able to easily or correctly determine which web sites to add to the cookie whitelist policy.

The example in Table 4 shows how to configure the policies under **Google\Google Chrome\Content Settings** to set the **Block cookies on these sites** and the **Allow cookies on these sites** policies to block cookies from all web sites except for those in the .gov and .mil domains. When these policies are configured they override the **Default cookies setting** policy if it has been enabled. This example is not meant as literal guidance.

Policy Name	Policy State	Policy Value
Block cookies on these sites	Enabled	*
Allow cookies on these sites	Enabled	[*.]gov [*.]mil

Table 4: Example policies for allowing cookies on specific web sites

---

[9] HTTP cookie. https://en.wikipedia.org/wiki/HTTP_cookie
[10] Cookies Allowed For Urls. http://www.chromium.org/administrators/policy-list-3#CookiesAllowedForUrls

Figure 5 shows the icon Chrome uses to notify a user that it has blocked cookies. A user can click on the blocked cookie icon to view more information about which specific cookies have been allowed and which specific cookies have been blocked.

Figure 5: The blocked cookie notification icon in the Chrome Omnibox

As an alternative to maintaining a cookie whitelist, administrators can configure Chrome to automatically delete all cookies when a user closes Chrome. Some enterprises may wish to keep all cookies on a system for forensics purposes while other enterprises may wish to have cookies deleted due to privacy and anonymity concerns. Setting the **Default cookies settings** policy to **Enabled** and its value to **Keep cookies for the duration of the session** is recommended if an enterprise doesn't need to retain cookies for forensic purposes. This is a new value for this policy in Chrome 21 that replaces the deprecated **Clear site data on browser shutdown** policy.

Third party cookies are web site cookies that come from a different web site than what the user is currently browsing. Advertising companies may often use third party cookies to track user activity across multiple web sites which can negatively impact user privacy and anonymity[9]. Setting the **Block third party cookies** policy to **Enabled** is recommended to block these types of cookies. The icon from Figure 5 also displays when third party cookies are blocked.

Unfortunately, a very small amount of web sites may not work correctly when third party cookies are blocked. In some cases the impact may be minor but in other cases this policy may prevent users from signing out of web sites. This issue may occur when a web site uses a different domain exclusively for handling the sign in or sign out process. This issue may confuse users since they may be under a false impression that they are completely and correctly signed out from a web site when they are not. Since the user may still be signed into a web site until the browser is closed, they may be signed in longer than desired which could be an operational security concern.

If an enterprise needs to retain cookies for forensics purposes or the policy negatively impacts user experience or operational security as already discussed, then the **Block third party cookies** policy should not be enabled. If this policy is enabled, then configuring the **Default cookies setting** policy as previously mentioned can be used to overcome the issue since all cookies will be deleted once the browser is closed.

3.7 JavaScript

JavaScript is commonly used by many web sites to enhance the user experience and often provides critical web site functionality. Chrome has the ability through policy to block JavaScript from running on all web sites. This is a secure but very restrictive setting which will break many web sites. Most users need JavaScript enabled to properly view and use web sites. It is possible to prevent JavaScript from running on all web sites and then selectively whitelist domains or web sites where JavaScript is allowed[5]. This is good security practice for security sensitive systems such as servers and administrative workstations. Applying this policy to all user workstations comes with an extremely high administrative overhead for managing the whitelist depending on the level of granularity used. Administrators should only apply this policy to all user workstations if users are not allowed to execute JavaScript or if administrators can quickly respond to user requests for adding web sites to the whitelist.

The example in Table 5 shows how to configure the policies under **Google\Google Chrome\Content Settings** to set the **Block Javascript on these sites** and the **Allow Javascript on these sites** policies to block JavaScript from running on all web sites except for those in the .gov and .mil domains. When these policies are configured they override the **Default Javascript setting** policy if it has been enabled. This example is not meant as literal guidance.

Policy Name	Policy State	Policy Value
Block Javascript on these sites	Enabled	*
Allow Javascript on these sites	Enabled	[*.]gov [*.]mil

Table 5: Example policies for allowing JavaScript to run on specific web sites

A more manageable option for user workstations is deploying a Chrome extension, such as ScriptNo, that blocks all JavaScript execution by default and allows the user to selectively enable JavaScript for the web sites they need to visit where JavaScript is essential for the web site to operate correctly. This option takes control away from administrators and places a significant amount of trust in the user to not enable JavaScript on malicious sites. Many users may require training to effectively use a JavaScript blocking extension without becoming frustrated and allowing all sites to execute JavaScript.

3.8 Plugins

Chrome supports a plugin architecture that allows it to display web content it does not natively support. Most plugins do not run in the Chrome sandbox. Plugins that are not sandboxed run under the privilege level of the user and have access to many system resources such as the file system and network. Allowing arbitrary plugins to execute will increase the overall attack surface of Chrome. An installation of Chrome includes several plugins by default as shown in Table 6.

Plugin Name	Description	Type	Sandboxed
Native Client	Executes native code in the browser. Used mostly for games.	PPAPI	Yes
Chrome Remote Desktop Viewer	Used for Chrome remote desktop also known as Chromoting. It was named **Remoting Viewer** in Chrome 21 and earlier versions.	PPAPI	Yes
Chrome PDF Viewer	Renders Adobe PDF files using the built-in sandboxed PDF viewer.	PPAPI	Yes
Shockwave Flash	Renders Adobe Flash content using an included Adobe Flash Player plugin. This plugin is only available by default in Chrome 21 and earlier versions.	NPAPI	No
Shockwave Flash	Renders Adobe Flash content using the Pepper Flash plugin. This plugin is only available by default in Chrome 21 and *later* versions.	PPAPI	Yes
Google Update	Uses Google Update to check for Chrome updates.	NPAPI	No

Table 6: Default plugins installed with Chrome

Blacklisting all plugins and then selectively whitelisting necessary plugins is recommended. This can be done by setting the **Specify a list of disabled plugins** policy to * to blacklist all plugins and then setting the **Specify a list of enabled plugins** policy to a list of plugin names that should be allowed. Whitelisting prevents users from running unauthorized plugins.

Common products[11] such as Oracle Java, Adobe Reader, RealPlayer, Apple QuickTime, and Microsoft Silverlight also install Chrome plugins to render their content. Table 7 contains a list of plugin names that can be used to whitelist plugins for common products.

Plugin Name(s)	Description	Type	Sandboxed
Adobe Acrobat	Renders Adobe PDF files in the browser.	NPAPI	No
Shockwave Flash	Renders Adobe Shockwave web content.	NPAPI	No
Apple QuickTime 7.7.2	Renders Apple audio and video web content.	NPAPI	No
Java Deployment Toolkit 7.0.50.255 Java(TM) Platform SE 7 U5	Allows web-based Java applications.	NPAPI	No
2007 Microsoft Office system	Renders Microsoft Office 2007 documents in the browser.	NPAPI	No
Microsoft Office 2010	Renders Microsoft Office 2010 documents in the browser.	NPAPI	No
Silverlight Plug-In	Renders Microsoft audio and video content in the browser.	NPAPI	No
RealPlayer(tm) G2 LiveConnect-Enabled Plug-In (32-bit) RealJukebox NS Plugin RealNetworks(tm) Chrome Background Extension Plug-In (32-bit)	Renders RealNetworks audio and video in the browser.	NPAPI	No

Table 7: Common plugins available for Chrome

Table 6 and Table 7 show the risk associated with enabling certain plugins. If the plugin uses the Netscape Plugin Application Programming Interface (NPAPI), then it is not sandboxed. If the plugin uses the Pepper Plugin Application Programming Interface (PPAPI), then it may be sandboxed. Sandboxed plugins should always be preferred over non-sandboxed plugins. As shown in Table 6 and Table 7, most common plugins are not sandboxed. Chrome added a sandboxed version of Adobe Flash starting with version 21 of Chrome and has included a sandboxed Adobe PDF reader plugin since version 8 of Chrome. Also note that only sandboxed plugins are allowed when running the Windows Store App, formerly known as Metro or Modern UI, version of Chrome in Windows 8 so no NPAPI plugins will work[12].

An administrator can view which plugins are available in Chrome by typing **chrome://plugins** in the Chrome Omnibox. Click the **Details** link on the right side of the Chrome plugins page to view plugin details such as the **Type** field, which indicates if the plugin uses NPAPI or PPAPI, the **Location** field, which displays the path of the executable that is used by the plugin, and the **Name** field, which can be used to whitelist the plugin.

When whitelisting plugins an administrator must use the exact spelling and letter casing displayed in the **Name** field for the specific plugin to be allowed. If the spelling or letter casing does not match, then the specific plugin will not be whitelisted. Some plugins have a version number in their plugin name that makes it more difficult to whitelist the plugin. The whitelisting policy supports using * and ? characters

---

[11] Chrome Plug-ins. http://support.google.com/chrome/bin/answer.py?hl=en&answer=142064

[12] NPAPI plug-ins in Windows 8 Metro mode. http://blog.chromium.org/2012/07/npapi-plug-ins-in-windows-8-metro-mode

as wildcard characters in the policy value. Use **QuickTime Plug-in*** or **QuickTime Plug-in ?.?.?** in the policy value to allow all versions of QuickTime plugins to run. Use ***Microsoft Office*** in the policy value to allow all versions of Microsoft Office plugins to run. Some products, such as Java and RealPlayer, may install multiple plugins for their content and all the plugins can be enabled or disabled using similar wildcard techniques.

In addition to whitelisting plugins, an administrator could also whitelist URLs that are allowed to run whitelisted plugins. For example, it is possible to configure Chrome so that the Adobe Flash plugin is only allowed to run on specific web sites. The example in Table 8 shows how to configure the policies under **Google\Google Chrome\Content Settings** to set the **Block Plugins on these sites** and the **Allow Plugins on these sites** policies to block plugins from running on all web sites except for those in the .gov and .mil domains. An administrator could also choose to further restrict plugins to only run on web sites that use HTTPS connections. When these policies are configured they override the **Default plugins setting** policy if it has been enabled. This example is not meant as literal guidance.

Policy Name	Policy State	Policy Value
Block Plugins on these sites	Enabled	*
Allow Plugins on these sites	Enabled	[*.]gov [*.]mil

Table 8: Example URL whitelist allowing plugins to run on specific web sites

Some Chrome plugins are automatically updated by an internal update mechanism that runs while Chrome is running. Chrome does not rely on Google Update to perform plugin updates. The NPAPI and PPAPI Flash plugins are examples of plugins that Chrome automatically updates. Chrome is not responsible for updating plugins, such as those shown in Table 7, that are installed by other products. Those plugins are typically updated by running the associated product's installer for the new version of the product.

Since setting the **Allow running plugins that are outdated** policy to **Disabled** is recommended, Chrome may automatically disable plugins that it detects as being outdated. This is done to protect the user from getting exploited due to viewing web content with outdated plugins that may contain known vulnerabilities. This is an important protection mechanism since most plugins are not sandboxed. Figure 6 shows an example of what a user will see on a web site when the plugin has been disabled due to enabling this policy. The content on the web site has been replaced by a notice which informs the user that the plugin has been disabled.

Figure 6: Web content for a plugin that has been disabled due to being outdated

Administrators can also view the status of plugins by typing **chrome://plugins** in the Chrome Omnibox. Click the **Details** link on the right side of the page. There will be a link labeled **Download Critical Security Update** near the plugin name for the associated plugin that has been disabled due to being outdated.

3.9 Extensions

Extensions are customization mechanisms that add extra features and functionality to the Chrome browser. Most, but not all, extensions can be downloaded via the Google Chrome Web Store[13]. Extensions can be written by anyone so caution should be used when determining which extensions are allowed to be installed in an enterprise. Using only extensions from the Google Chrome Web Store does not guarantee safety since Google does not author many of the extensions. Despite the risks, extensions are usually much less risky than plugins since extensions usually do not have full access to the system like most plugins do. Allowing extensions can have both usability and security benefits, but always keep in mind the amount and type of data an extension can access and where an extension may send data.

Extensions request a level of permission which grants them access to certain resources in the browser. Google categorizes the permissions into three levels of risk which are displayed in Table 9.

	Risk	Extension Permissions
	High	Access all data on the computer and web sites you visit. It could use the web cam or read and write files.
	Medium	Access your data on all web sites you visit.
	Low	Access your bookmarks, history, clipboard data, physical location, open tabs, extension list.

Table 9: Chrome extension risk categorization based on permissions

Extensions that request access to **All data on your computer and web sites you visit** are highly privileged extensions that can do almost anything inside or outside the browser. High risk extensions contain NPAPI plugins and do not run in the sandbox. Avoiding installation of high risk extensions, unless absolutely necessary, is recommended. More information about extensions and their risks can be found in Appendix C.

While Google categorizes extensions at a particular risk level based on the browser or operating system resources the extension accesses, the risk in allowing an extension should also take into consideration the operational security needs of the network rather than only relying on Google's risk categorization. For example, Google categorizes extensions that access your physical location, based on geolocation information, as a low risk. The operational security needs of one network may categorize geolocation as a high risk while another network may categorize geolocation as a medium risk.

An administrator can check the permissions an extension requires by viewing the extension's Details page on the Chrome Web Store. See Figure 7 for an example of a high risk extension.

---

[13] Chrome Web Store – Extensions. https://chrome.google.com/webstore/category/extensions

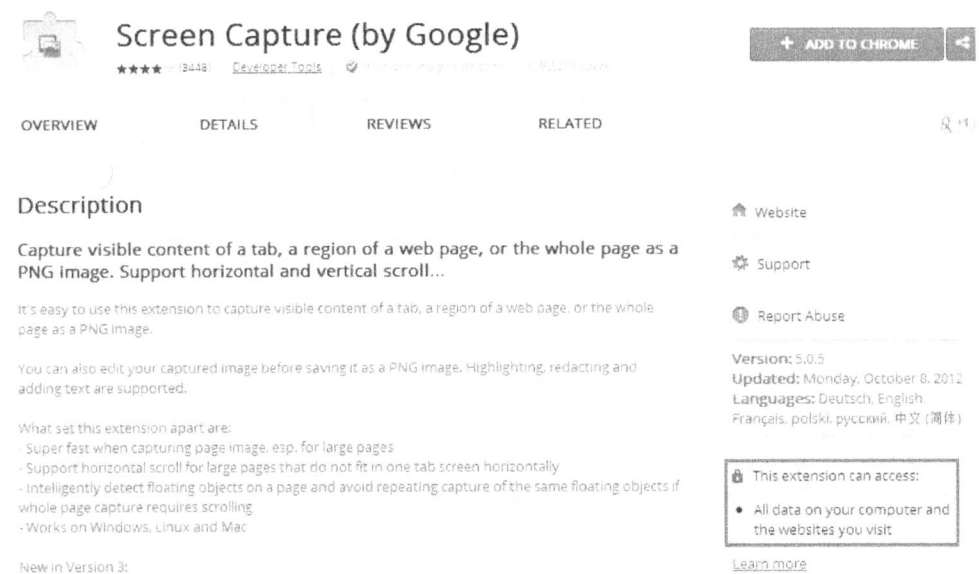

Figure 7: Example of a high risk extension in the Chrome Web Store

Extension permissions are also displayed in the Confirm New Extension dialog when a user installs an extension as shown in Figure 8.

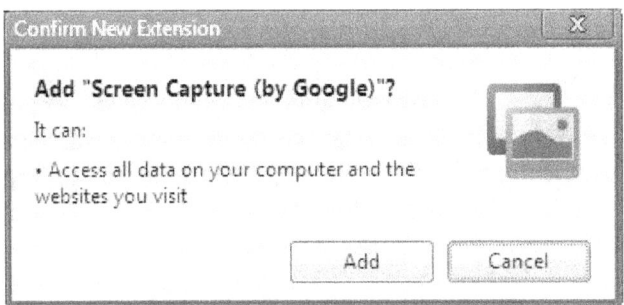

Figure 8: Chrome extension installation prompt displaying a permission warning

If an administrator allows extensions, then blacklisting all extensions by setting the **Configure extension installation blacklist** policy to * and then selectively whitelisting approved extensions is recommended. Extensions can be whitelisted by adding the extension ID to the **Configure extension installation whitelist** policy. Table 10 shows some example extensions. It is common for many extensions to be categorized as a medium risk when using Google's risk categorization.

Extension Name	Extension ID	Sandboxed	Risk
Google SSL Web Search	lcncmkcnkcdbbanbjakcencbaoegdjlp	Yes	Low
AdBlock	gighmmpiobklfepjocnamgkkbiglidom	Yes	Medium
Do Not Track	ckdcpbflcbeillmamogkpmdhnbeggfja	Yes	Medium
Flash Block	gofhjkjmkpinhpoiabjplobcaignabnl	Yes	Medium
HTTPS Everywhere	gcbommkclmclpchllfjekcdonpmejbdp	Yes	Medium
Disconnect	jeoacafpbcihiomhlakeieifhpjdfeo	Yes	Medium
Ghostery	mlomiejdfkolichcfleclcbmpeanij	Yes	Medium
ScriptNo	oiiigbmnaadbkfbmpbfijlflahbdbdgdf	Yes	Medium
Screen Capture (by Google)	cpngackimfmofbokmjmljamhdncknpmg	No	High

Table 10: Example Chrome extensions

Administrators can find an extension's ID by viewing the extension in the Chrome Web Store and looking at the string of characters at the end of the URL. See Figure 9 for an example of a URL containing an extension ID. Administrators can also view extension IDs in Chrome by typing **chrome://extensions** in the Chrome Omnibox and observing the **Extension ID** field value for each installed extension.

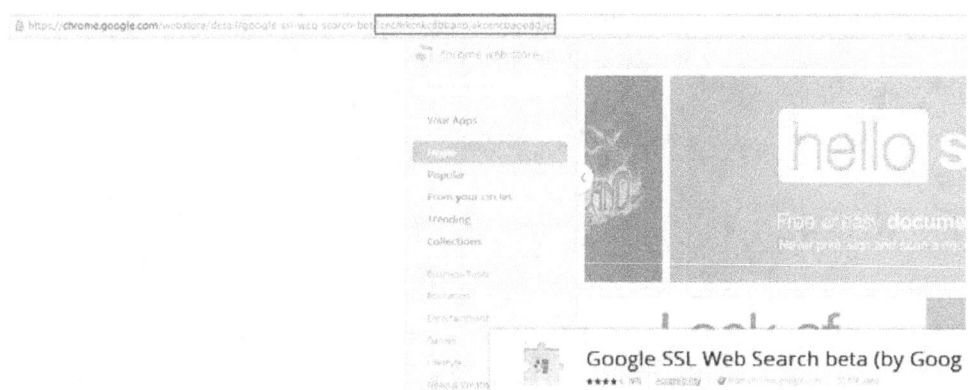

Figure 9: An extension ID in a Chrome Web Store URL

Enterprise deployment of extensions can be done through policy by forcing extension installation. The example in Table 11 shows how to configure the policy under **Google\Google Chrome\Extensions** to set the **Configure the list of force-installed extensions** policy to deploy two extensions. The example contains the extension IDs for ScriptNo and the HTTPS Everywhere extensions.

Policy Value
oiigbmnaadbkfbmpbfijlflahbdbdgdf;https://clients2.google.com/service/update2/crx
gcbommkclmclpchllfjekcdonpmejbdp;https://www.eff.org/files/https-everywhere-chrome-updates.xml

Table 11: Example values for the force install extensions policy

For each extension that needs to be deployed to the enterprise, add an item to the policy value that contains an extension ID and an extension update URL separated by a semicolon. The extension will be silently installed the next time Chrome starts. Remove the item from the **Configure the list of force-installed extensions** policy and the extension will be silently uninstalled the next time Chrome starts.

The extension ID can also optionally be added to the **Configure extension installation whitelist** policy, since extension whitelisting is recommended, but force-installed extensions are essentially whitelisted even if the extension is not specified in the whitelist policy. Adding all the extension IDs of the force-installed extensions to the whitelist policy is recommended to keep track of all approved extensions in one location.

All extensions installed from the Chrome Web Store expect the extension update URL to be **https://clients2.google.com/service/update2/crx**. Extensions from outside the Chrome Web Store that support automatic updates expect a URL to the XML file which contains automatic update information for the extension. This URL can be obtained by extracting the extension's **manifest.json** file and then using the value of the **update_url** field in the policy. If the manifest does not contain that field, then the extension does not support automatic updates.

Chrome is responsible for performing periodic extension update checks through an internal update mechanism rather than using the Google Update service. Chrome will automatically and silently install extension updates when new versions of extensions become available. Extensions from the Chrome Web Store will always get automatically updated but extensions from other sources will only get updated if the extension supports it as noted in the previous paragraph. Starting with Chrome 21, extensions installed from sources other than the Chrome Web Store may need their web site URLs added to the **Configure extension, app, and user script install sources** policy.

4 Google Update

Chrome automatically updates on a regular basis by using the Google Update service that is installed with Chrome. Google Update is separate from Chrome and is based on the open source Omaha project[14]. Google uses the Google Update service to update other Google products, such as Google Earth, when they are installed on a system. Google Update will only be uninstalled from a system once the last Google product that uses Google Update is uninstalled from the system.

Google Update uses different update strategies depending on the configuration of the system. The main update strategy uses the Windows Task Scheduler service. Two scheduled tasks, shown in Figure 10, are created during Chrome installation to perform update checks. One scheduled task runs an update check once every 24 hours. The other scheduled task runs an update check on user login and repeats the update check every hour for 24 hours. The tasks may not be visible unless logged into the system as an administrator.

Name	Status	Triggers	Author
GoogleUpdateTaskMachineCore1cd6...	Ready	Multiple triggers defined	SYSTEM
GoogleUpdateTaskMachineUA	Ready	At 4:34 PM every day - After triggered, repeat every 1 hour for a duration of 1 day.	SYSTEM

Figure 10: Windows scheduled tasks for the Google Update service

If the individual scheduled tasks are disabled or the Windows Task Scheduler service is disabled, then the Google Update service uses its own services, as shown in Figure 11, to perform updates. The Google Update service runs an internal scheduler process that performs an update check every 24 hours.

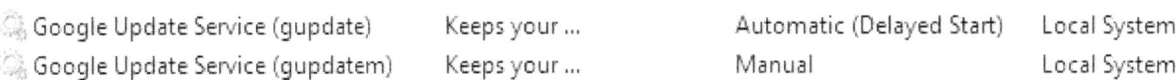

| Google Update Service (gupdate) | Keeps your ... | Automatic (Delayed Start) | Local System |
| Google Update Service (gupdatem) | Keeps your ... | Manual | Local System |

Figure 11: Windows services for the Google Update service

---

[14] Omaha software installer and auto-updater for Windows. http://code.google.com/omaha

Administrators can download and import the Google Update Administrative Template[15] to disable Google Update through Group Policy. Once the template has been imported, an administrator can completely disable Google Update:

1. Navigate to **Computer Configuration > Policies > Administrative Templates > Classic Administrative Templates (ADM) > Google > Google Update > Preferences**.
2. Set the **Auto-update check period override** policy to **Enabled**
3. Set the **Minutes between update checks** value to **0**.
4. Select the **Disable all auto-update checks (not recommended)** checkbox.

This will result in creation of a DWORD registry value named **AutoUpdateCheckPeriodMinutes** with its value set to **0** and another DWORD registry value named **DisableAutoUpdateChecksCheckboxValue** with its value set to **1** under the registry key of **HKLM\Software\Policies\Google\Update**. If an administrator does not want to use the Google Update Administrative Template, then create that registry value on all systems. Despite setting this policy to disable Chrome updates, the Google Update service may still attempt to update itself.

The Google Update services can be completely disabled which will prevent Google Update from updating itself in addition to preventing Chrome from updating. To disable the Google Update services, stop the services in the Service Control Manager or navigate to **HKLM\System\CurrentControlSet\Services** and set the DWORD value named **Start** to a value of **4** for the **gpupdate** and **gpupdatem** services.

There is also a Google Update Chrome plugin named Google Update, as previously shown in Table 6, which is installed and registered in Chrome by default. The Google Update plugin can be disabled by leaving its name out of the **Specify a list of enabled plugins** policy, as previously discussed in the Plugins section, so that the plugin is not whitelisted. Note that Chrome still automatically updates some of its plugins, extensions, and certificate revocation data on its own regardless of these policies.

As previously discussed, some enterprises may wish to disable automatic updates in favor of manually deploying updates. These enterprises can use their preferred software update mechanism, or use Group Policy software installation as mentioned in the Deployment section, to publish the updated Chrome MSI to their systems. Even though this section explains how to disable automatic updates so administrators can use their preferred deployment method, leaving automatic updates enabled to keep Chrome fully patched and protected from known vulnerabilities is strongly recommended unless an enterprise is prepared to keep pace with the frequency that Chrome stable channel updates are released which is approximately every 2 weeks.

Keeping software patched and updated is an important practice for an enterprise to protect itself from malicious activity. Appendix D contains PowerShell scripts that can be used to check an entire Windows domain and report computers that are not running the latest version of Chrome.

---

[15] Google Update for Enterprise. http://support.google.com/installer/bin/answer.py?hl=en&answer=146164

5 Appendix

5.1 Appendix A: Binaries Installed by Chrome

This appendix contains information about the security attributes, such as Data Execution Prevention (DEP), Address Space Layout Randomization (ASLR), of the binaries installed with Chrome and Google Update and the entity that digitally signed the binary. See Table 12 and Table 13 for this information. These tables list the binaries installed by the Chrome 22 MSI.

File Name	DEP	ASLR	Digitally Signed By
avcodec-54.dll	Yes	Yes	Google Inc
avformat-54.dll	Yes	Yes	Google Inc
avutil-51.dll	Yes	Yes	Google Inc
chrome.dll	Yes	Yes	Google Inc
chrome_frame_helper.dll	Yes	Yes	Google Inc
chrome_frame_helper.exe	Yes	Yes	Google Inc
chrome_launcher.exe	Yes	Yes	Google Inc
d3dcompiler_43.dll	Yes	Yes	Microsoft Corporation
d3dx9_43.dll	Yes	Yes	Microsoft Corporation
delegate_execute.exe	Yes	Yes	Google Inc
icudt.dll	Yes	Yes	Google Inc
libegl.dll	Yes	Yes	Google Inc
libglesv2.dll	Yes	Yes	Google Inc
metro_driver.dll	Yes	Yes	Google Inc
nacl64.exe	Yes	Yes	Google Inc
npchrome_frame.dll	Yes	Yes	Google Inc
pdf.dll	Yes	Yes	Google Inc
ppgooglenaclpluginchrome.dll	Yes	Yes	Google Inc
xinput1_3.dll	No	No	Microsoft Corporation
chrome.exe	Yes	Yes	Google Inc
pepflashplayer.dll	Yes	Yes	Google Inc

Table 12: Binaries for Chrome

Prior to Google Update version 1.3, GoogleUpdate.exe was not compiled with ASLR. Administrators should ensure their systems have the latest version of GoogleUpdate installed.

File Name	DEP	ASLR	Digitally Signed By
GoogleUpdate.exe	Yes	Yes	Google Inc
GoogleUpdateBroker.exe	Yes	Yes	Google Inc
GoogleUpdateCrashHandler.exe	Yes	Yes	Google Inc
GoogleUpdateCrashHandler64.exe	Yes	Yes	Google Inc
GoogleUpdateOnDemand.exe	Yes	Yes	Google Inc
goopdate.dll	Yes	Yes	Google Inc
goopdateres_xx.dll	Yes	Yes	Google Inc
npGoogleUpdate3.dll	Yes	Yes	Google Inc
psmachine.dll	Yes	Yes	Google Inc
psuser.dll	Yes	Yes	Google Inc

Table 13: Binaries for Google Update

Administrators can also use the Microsoft Enhanced Mitigations Experience Toolkit (EMET)[16] to add Mandatory ASLR and other additional protections to Chrome and Google Update executables. EMET 3.0

---

[16] Microsoft Enhanced Mitigations Experience Toolkit. http://support.microsoft.com/kb/2458544

was tested with Chrome and Google Update executables and no incompatibilities were found with any of the protections provided by EMET. Configuring Microsoft EMET to protect executables that perform network communication or process untrusted data is recommended to provide an additional layer of defense against exploits.

5.2 Appendix B: Chrome Policy Registry Data

This appendix contains information administrators can use to verify that Chrome Group Policy settings have been applied to their systems as intended. Administrators can use registry viewing tools to observe the registry keys and registry values created after Group Policy updates have been processed on a system. The policies in this guide are configured within the Computer Configuration section of Group Policy under the **Google Chrome** folder. These policies will create registry keys and values on systems under the registry key path of **HKLM\Software\Policies\Google\Chrome**.

5.2.1 Mapping Policy Names to Registry Data

Table 14 contains a mapping of Chrome browser Group Policy names to their registry key names or registry value names as of Chrome 22. The table does not contain any policies that have been deprecated since those policies will be removed in future Chrome releases. The table also does not contain policies related Google Chrome Frame or Chrome OS. Entries in the Registry Value Name or Key Name column that end with a slash are registry key names. Entries in the Registry Value Name or Key Name column that do not end with a slash are registry value names.

Chrome Policy Name	Registry Value Name or Key Name	Type
Enable firewall traversal from remote access host	RemoteAccessHostFirewallTraversal	REG_DWORD
Configure the required domain name for remote access hosts	RemoteAccessHostDomain	REG_SZ
Enable two-factor authentication for remote access hosts	RemoteAccessHostRequireTwoFactor	REG_DWORD
Configure the TalkGadget prefix for remote access hosts	RemoteAccessHostTalkGadgetPrefix	REG_SZ
Default cookies setting	DefaultCookiesSetting	REG_DWORD
Default images setting	DefaultImagesSetting	REG_DWORD
Default JavaScript setting	DefaultJavaScriptSetting	REG_DWORD
Default plugins setting	DefaultPluginsSetting	REG_DWORD
Default popups setting	DefaultPopupsSetting	REG_DWORD
Default notification setting	DefaultNotificationsSetting	REG_DWORD
Default geolocation setting	DefaultGeolocationSetting	REG_DWORD
Default mediastream setting	DefaultMediaStreamSetting	REG_DWORD
Automatically select client certificates for these sites	AutoSelectCertificateForUrls\	REG_SZ
Allow cookies on these sites	CookiesAllowedForUrls\	REG_SZ
Block cookies on these sites	CookiesBlockedForUrls\	REG_SZ
Allow session only cookies on these sites	CookiesSessionOnlyForUrls\	REG_SZ
Allow images on these sites	ImagesAllowedForUrls\	REG_SZ
Block images on these sites	ImagesBlockedForUrls\	REG_SZ
Allow JavaScript on these sites	JavaScriptAllowedForUrls\	REG_SZ
Block JavaScript on these sites	JavaScriptBlockedForUrls\	REG_SZ
Allow plugins on these sites	PluginsAllowedForUrls\	REG_SZ
Block plugins on these sites	PluginsBlockedForUrls\	REG_SZ
Allow popups on these sites	PopupsAllowedForUrls\	REG_SZ
Block popups on these sites	PopupsBlockedForUrls\	REG_SZ
Allow notifications on these sites	NotificationsAllowedForUrls\	REG_SZ
Block notifications on these sites	NotificationsBlockedForUrls\	REG_SZ
Enable the default search provider	DefaultSearchProviderEnabled	REG_DWORD

Chrome Policy Name	Registry Value Name or Key Name	Type
Default search provider name	DefaultSearchProviderName	REG_SZ
Default search provider keyword	DefaultSearchProviderKeyword	REG_SZ
Default search provider search URL	DefaultSearchProviderSearchURL	REG_SZ
Default search provider suggest URL	DefaultSearchProviderSuggestURL	REG_SZ
Default search provider instant URL	DefaultSearchProviderInstantURL	REG_SZ
Default search provider icon	DefaultSearchProviderIconURL	REG_SZ
Default search provider encodings	DefaultSearchProviderEncodings\	REG_SZ
Configure extension installation blacklist	ExtensionInstallBlacklist\	REG_SZ
Configure extension installation whitelist	ExtensionInstallWhitelist\	REG_SZ
Configure the list of force-installed extensions	ExtensionInstallForcelist\	REG_SZ
Configure extension, app, and user script install sources	ExtensionInstallSources\	REG_SZ
Configure the home page URL	HomepageLocation	REG_SZ
Use New Tab Page as homepage	HomepageIsNewTabPage	REG_DWORD
Enable the password manager	PasswordManagerEnabled	REG_DWORD
Allow users to show passwords in Password Manager	PasswordManagerAllowShowPasswords	REG_DWORD
Supported authentication schemes	AuthSchemes	REG_SZ
Disable CNAME lookup when negotiating Kerberos authentication	DisableAuthNegotiateCnameLookup	REG_DWORD
Include non-standard port in Kerberos SPN	EnableAuthNegotiatePort	REG_DWORD
Authentication server whitelist	AuthServerWhitelist	REG_SZ
Kerberos delegation server whitelist	AuthNegotiateDelegateWhitelist	REG_SZ
Cross-origin HTTP Basic Auth prompts	AllowCrossOriginAuthPrompt	REG_DWORD
Choose how to specify proxy server settings	ProxyMode	REG_SZ
Address or URL of proxy server	ProxyServer	REG_SZ
URL to a proxy .pac file	ProxyPacUrl	REG_SZ
Proxy bypass rules	ProxyBypassList	REG_SZ
Action on startup	RestoreOnStartup	REG_DWORD
URLs to open on startup	RestoreOnStartupURLs\	REG_SZ
Allow invocation of file selection dialogs	AllowFileSelectionDialogs	REG_DWORD
Allow running plugins that are outdated	AllowOutdatedPlugins	REG_DWORD
Enable alternate error pages	AlternateErrorPagesEnabled	REG_DWORD
Always runs plugins that require authorization	AlwaysAuthorizePlugins	REG_DWORD
Application locale	ApplicationLocaleValue	REG_SZ
Enable AutoFill	AutoFillEnabled	REG_DWORD
Continue running background apps when Google Chrome is closed	BackgroundModeEnabled	REG_DWORD
Block third party cookies	BlockThirdPartyCookies	REG_DWORD
Enable Bookmark Bar	BookmarkBarEnabled	REG_DWORD
Enable Google Cloud Print proxy	CloudPrintProxyEnabled	REG_DWORD
Enable submission of documents to Google Cloud Print	CloudPrintSubmitEnabled	REG_DWORD
Set Chrome as Default Browser	DefaultBrowserSettingEnabled	REG_DWORD
Disable Developer Tools	DeveloperToolsDisabled	REG_DWORD
Disable support for 3D graphics APIs	Disable3DAPIs	REG_DWORD
Specify whether the plugin finder should be disabled	DisablePluginFinder	REG_DWORD
Disable Print Preview	DisablePrintPreview	REG_DWORD
Disable SSL record splitting	DisableSSLRecordSplitting	REG_DWORD
Disable proceeding from the Safe Browsing warning page	DisableSafeBrowsingProceedAnyway	REG_DWORD
Disable taking screenshots	DisableScreenshots	REG_DWORD
Disable SPDY protocol	DisableSpdy	REG_DWORD
Specify a list of disabled plugins	DisabledPlugins\	REG_SZ
Specify a list of plugins that the user can enable or disable	DisabledPluginsExceptions\	REG_SZ
Disable URL protocol schemes	DisabledSchemes\	REG_SZ
Set disk cache directory	DiskCacheDir	REG_SZ
Set disk cache size in bytes	DiskCacheSize	REG_DWORD

Chrome Policy Name	Registry Value Name or Key Name	Type
Enable network prediction	DnsPrefetchingEnabled	REG_DWORD
Set download directory	DownloadDirectory	REG_SZ
Enables or disables bookmark editing	EditBookmarksEnabled	REG_DWORD
Whether online OCSP/CRL checks are performed	EnableOnlineRevocationChecks	REG_DWORD
Specify a list of enabled plugins	EnabledPlugins\	REG_SZ
Enterprise web store name	EnterpriseWebStoreName	REG_SZ
Enterprise web store URL	EnterpriseWebStoreURL	REG_SZ
Import bookmarks from default browser on first run	ImportBookmarks	REG_DWORD
Import browsing history from default browser on first run	ImportHistory	REG_DWORD
Import of homepage from default browser on first run	ImportHomepage	REG_DWORD
Import saved passwords from default browser on first run	ImportSavedPasswords	REG_DWORD
Import search engines from default browser on first run	ImportSearchEngine	REG_DWORD
Incognito mode availability	IncognitoModeAvailability	REG_DWORD
Enable Instant	InstantEnabled	REG_DWORD
Maximal number of concurrent connections to the proxy server	MaxConnectionsPerProxy	REG_DWORD
Set media disk cache size in bytes	MediaCacheSize	REG_DWORD
Enable reporting of usage and crash-related data	MetricsReportingEnabled	REG_DWORD
Enable printing	PrintingEnabled	REG_DWORD
Restrict which users are allowed to sign in to Google Chrome	RestrictSigninToPattern	REG_SZ
Enable Safe Browsing	SafeBrowsingEnabled	REG_DWORD
Disable saving browser history	SavingBrowserHistoryDisabled	REG_DWORD
Enable search suggestions	SearchSuggestEnabled	REG_DWORD
Show Home button on toolbar	ShowHomeButton	REG_DWORD
Enable or disable spell checking web service	SpellCheckServiceEnabled	REG_DWORD
Disable synchronization of data with Google	SyncDisabled	REG_DWORD
Enable Translate	TranslateEnabled	REG_DWORD
Block access to a list of URLs	URLBlacklist\	REG_SZ
Allows access to a list of URLs	URLWhitelist\	REG_SZ
Set user data directory	UserDataDir	REG_SZ

Table 14: Mapping of Chrome Group Policy names to registry key or value names

5.2.2 Example Policy Registry Data

Most Chrome policies only generate registry values. Some Chrome policies that accept lists of data create a specific registry key and numbered registry value names below it. The **Configure extension installation blacklist** policy accepts a list of extension IDs and the table's entry for the policy denotes that it creates a registry key name since it ends with a slash. Setting the policy value to * creates a registry key name of **ExtensionInstallBlacklist** with a REG_SZ registry value name of **1** below it whose value data is set to *. The data extracted by the Windows Registry Editor will look as shown below.

```
Windows Registry Editor Version 5.00

[HKEY_LOCAL_MACHINE\SOFTWARE\Policies\Google\Chrome\ExtensionInstallBlacklist]
"1"="*"
```

The **Configure extension installation whitelist** creates a registry key name of **ExtensionInstallWhitelist**. When the policy value is configured to allow two extensions, then two REG_SZ registry values, named **1** and **2**, are created below the **ExtensionInstallWhitelist** registry key name. The data extracted by the Windows Registry Editor will look as shown below.

```
Windows Registry Editor Version 5.00

[HKEY_LOCAL_MACHINE\SOFTWARE\Policies\Google\Chrome\ExtensionInstallWhitelist]
```

```
1 = "lcncmkcnkcdbbanbjakcencbaoegdjlp"
2 = "gcbommkclmclpchllfjekcdonpmejbdp"
```

Most Chrome policies that accept lists of data generate registry data in the above format and are noted in Table 14 by having the Registry Value Name or Key Name column ending with a slash character. Notable exceptions are the **Supported authentication schemes**, **Authentication server whitelist**, and **Kerberos delegation server whitelist** policies. These policies only generate a single registry value name and use a REG_SZ registry data type that stores a comma delimited string as its registry value data.

The rest of this appendix shows extracted registry data generated by Chrome policy templates to illustrate the policies discussed in this guide. Registry data corresponding to the recommended policies in Table 1 are included below.

```
Windows Registry Editor Version 5.00

[HKEY_LOCAL_MACHINE\SOFTWARE\Policies\Google\Chrome]
"AllowOutdatedPlugins"=dword:00000000
"AlwaysAuthorizePlugins"=dword:00000000
"DisablePluginFinder"=dword:00000001
"RemoteAccessHostFirewallTraversal"=dword:00000000
"DefaultGeolocationSetting"=dword:00000002
"DefaultNotificationsSetting"=dword:00000002
"DefaultPopupsSetting"=dword:00000002
"PasswordManagerAllowShowPasswords"=dword:00000000
"PasswordManagerEnabled"=dword:00000000
"AuthSchemes"="negotiate"
"BackgroundModeEnabled"=dword:00000000
"SavingBrowserHistoryDisabled"=dword:00000000
"DisableSpdy"=dword:00000001
"Disable3DAPIs"=dword:00000001
"SyncDisabled"=dword:00000001
"AutoFillEnabled"=dword:00000000
"CloudPrintProxyEnabled"=dword:00000000
"InstantEnabled"=dword:00000000
"DnsPrefetchingEnabled"=dword:00000000
"MetricsReportingEnabled"=dword:00000000
"SafeBrowsingEnabled"=dword:00000001
"SearchSuggestEnabled"=dword:00000000
"CloudPrintSubmitEnabled"=dword:00000000
"ImportSavedPasswords"=dword:00000000
"EnableOnlineRevocationChecks"=dword:00000001
"IncognitoModeAvailability"=dword:00000001
"DefaultMediaStreamSetting"=dword:00000002
"DisableSafeBrowsingProceedAnyway"=dword:00000001
"DisableScreenshots"=dword:00000001


[HKEY_LOCAL_MACHINE\SOFTWARE\Policies\Google\Chrome\DisabledPlugins]
"1"="*"


[HKEY_LOCAL_MACHINE\SOFTWARE\Policies\Google\Chrome\DisabledSchemes]
"1"="file"
"2"="javascript"


[HKEY_LOCAL_MACHINE\SOFTWARE\Policies\Google\Chrome\EnabledPlugins]
"1"="Shockwave Flash"
"2"="Chrome PDF Viewer"


[HKEY_LOCAL_MACHINE\SOFTWARE\Policies\Google\Chrome\ExtensionInstallBlacklist]
"1"="*"
```

Registry data for the optional example policies in the User Settings and User Cache Location section are included below.

```
Windows Registry Editor Version 5.00

[HKEY_LOCAL_MACHINE\SOFTWARE\Policies\Google\Chrome]
"DiskCacheDir"="${local_app_data}\\Chrome"
"UserDataDir"="${roaming_app_data}\\Chrome"
```

Registry data for the optional example policies corresponding to Table 3 in the Default Search Provider section are included below.

```
Windows Registry Editor Version 5.00

[HKEY_LOCAL_MACHINE\SOFTWARE\Policies\Google\Chrome]
"DefaultSearchProviderName"="Google Encrypted Search"
"DefaultSearchProviderSearchURL"="https://encrypted.google.com/search?{google:acceptedSuggestion}{google:originalQueryForSuggestion}sourceid=
chrome&ie={inputEncoding}&q={searchTerms}"
"DefaultSearchProviderEnabled"=dword:00000001
```

Registry data for the optional example policies corresponding to Table 4 in the Cookies section are included below.

```
Windows Registry Editor Version 5.00

 [HKEY_LOCAL_MACHINE\SOFTWARE\Policies\Google\Chrome\CookiesAllowedForUrls]
"1"="[*.]gov"
"2"="[*.]mil"

[HKEY_LOCAL_MACHINE\SOFTWARE\Policies\Google\Chrome\CookiesBlockedForUrls]
"1"="*"
```

Registry data for the optional, but recommended if possible, policies in the Cookies section are included below.

```
Windows Registry Editor Version 5.00

[HKEY_LOCAL_MACHINE\SOFTWARE\Policies\Google\Chrome]
"BlockThirdPartyCookies"=dword:00000001
"DefaultCookiesSetting"=dword:00000004
```

Registry data for the optional example policies corresponding to Table 5 in the JavaScript section are included below.

```
Windows Registry Editor Version 5.00

 [HKEY_LOCAL_MACHINE\SOFTWARE\Policies\Google\Chrome\JavaScriptAllowedForUrls]
"1"="[*.]gov"
"2"="[*.]mil"

[HKEY_LOCAL_MACHINE\SOFTWARE\Policies\Google\Chrome\JavaScriptBlockedForUrls]
"1"="*"
```

Registry data for the optional example policies corresponding to Table 8 in the Plugins section are included below.

```
Windows Registry Editor Version 5.00

[HKEY_LOCAL_MACHINE\SOFTWARE\Policies\Google\Chrome\PluginsAllowedForUrls]
"1"="[*.]gov"
"2"="[*.]mil"

[HKEY_LOCAL_MACHINE\SOFTWARE\Policies\Google\Chrome\PluginsBlockedForUrls]
"1"="*"
```

Registry data for an example extension whitelisting policy combining policies from Table 1 in the Policies section and some extensions from Table 10 in the Extensions section are included below. The extensions used in this example are Google SSL Web Search, Do Not Track, AdBlock, Flash Block, HTTPS Everywhere, Disconnect, Ghostery, and ScriptNo.

```
Windows Registry Editor Version 5.00

[HKEY_LOCAL_MACHINE\SOFTWARE\Policies\Google\Chrome\ExtensionInstallBlacklist]
"1"="*"
```

```
[HKEY_LOCAL_MACHINE\SOFTWARE\Policies\Google\Chrome\ExtensionInstallWhitelist]
"1"="lcncmkcnkcdbbanbjakcencbaoegdjlp"
"2"="ckdcpbflcbeillmamogkpmdhnbeggfja"
"3"="gighmmpiobklfepjocnamgkkbiglidom"
"4"="gofhjkjmkpinhpoiabjplobcaignabnl"
"5"="gcbommkclmclpchllfjekcdonpmejbdp"
"6"="jeoacafpbcihiomhlakeieifhpjdfeo"
"7"="mlomiejdfkolichcfleclcbmpeanij"
"8"="oiigbmnaadbkfbmpbfijlflahbdbdgdf"
```

The above examples, combined with Table 14 in this appendix, should assist administrators in confirming that Chrome policies are applied to systems as expected.

5.3 Appendix C: Chrome Extension Permissions and Warnings

This appendix contains more detailed information about Chrome extensions, their permissions, and their associated warning messages. Most of the information is from Chrome documentation with some additional information to help administrators determine risks associated with an extension and to help understand actions an extension may perform.

Chrome extension permissions can be broken down using a number of risk categories. Some extensions may display a warning message that can be mapped to a particular risk category[17]. High level descriptions and examples are given below with more details given in Table 15.

High risk

Extensions containing high risk permissions are not sandboxed and can access any resource that the user can access. Extensions requiring this permission level should be avoided unless absolutely necessary.

- **Access all data on your computer and the web sites you visit**. This extension contains an NPAPI plug-in.
  Caution: NPAPI plug-ins can do almost anything, in or outside of your browser. For example, they could use your webcam, or they could read your personal files.

Medium risk

Extensions using medium risk permissions are sandboxed, can access all the data on a web site, and can modify data on the web site on your behalf. It is common for most extensions to be considered medium risk.

- **Access your data on all web sites**. This extension can read every page that you visit -- your bank, your web email, your Facebook page, and so on. This kind of extension needs to see all pages so that it can perform a limited task such as looking for RSS feeds that you might want to subscribe to.
  Caution: Besides seeing all your pages, this extension could use your credentials (cookies) to request or modify your data from web sites.
- **Access your data on *{list of web sites}***. This extension can read the pages that you visit on the specified web sites.

---

[17] Permissions requested by apps and extensions. http://support.google.com/chrome_webstore/bin/answer.py?hl=en&answer=186213

Caution: Besides seeing all your pages, this extension could use your credentials (cookies) to request or modify your data from web sites.

Low risk

Extensions using low risk permissions are sandboxed and can access specific types of information. What Google categorizes as low risk may or may not be a low risk depending on the operational security needs of the network.

- **Manage your apps, extensions, and themes**. This extension can read the list of themes, extensions, and apps that you have installed. It can't install an extension, but it might enable, disable, uninstall, or launch an extension that you've installed.
- **Read and modify your bookmarks**. This extension can read, change, add to, and organize your bookmarks.
- **Read and modify your browsing history**. This extension can look at and erase your browsing history.
- **Access your tabs and browsing activity**. This extension can see the addresses and titles of web sites that you visit in tabs and windows. This warning might be a by-product of an extension needing to open new tabs or windows.
- **Detect your physical location**. This extension uses location information that your computer provides about where you currently are.
- **Access data you copy and paste**. This extension can read data that you copy into your operating system clipboard, which might include sensitive or private information. An example of possibly sensitive information on the clipboard is a phone number that you copy from a web site or from a local document.

No warning

Certain types of extension permissions do not have an associated warning message. This does not mean there is no risk associated with the permission but there will be no warning message displayed when installing an extension that only uses permissions that have no associated warning message.

? Uncategorized risk

Some permissions display messages that have not been categorized by Google yet so they only have suggested risk levels.

- **Manipulate settings that specify whether web sites can use features such as cookies, JavaScript, and plug-ins**. This extension can customize Chrome's behavior on a per-site basis to change settings that control whether web sites can use features such as cookies, JavaScript, and plug-ins. Suggested risk: **Medium**.
- **Access the content of the pages you visit**. This extension can save a page's content as MHTML. Suggested risk: **Low**.
- **Manipulate privacy-related settings**. This extension can to control usage of the features in Chrome that can affect a user's privacy. Suggested risk: **Medium**.
- **Page debugger backend**. This extension can allow remote debugging of a Chrome tab. Suggested risk: **High**.

- **Access your data on chrome://favicon**. This extension can control which favicon is displayed for a web site. Suggested risk: **Low**.
- **Access all text spoken using synthesized speech**. This extension can implement a text to speech engine. Suggested risk: **Low**.

The data in Table 15 maps a corresponding Chrome extension risk level to a warning message and the associated permission entry in the extension's manifest.json file[18].

Risk	Warning Message	Permission	Description
✓	None	background	Makes Chrome start up early and shut down late so that apps and extensions can have a longer life.
	Read and modify your bookmarks	bookmarks	Allows creation, organization, and manipulation of bookmarks. Required if the extension uses the chrome.bookmarks module.
✓	None	browsingData	Allows an extension to remove browsing data from a user's profile. Required if the extension uses the chrome.browsingData module.
?	Access your data on favicon	chrome://favicon	Required if the extension uses the *chrome://favicon/url* mechanism to display the favicon of a page.
	Access data you copy and paste	clipboardRead	Required if the extension uses document.execCommand('paste').
✓	None	clipboardWrite	Required if the extension uses document.execCommand('copy') or document.execCommand('cut').
?	Manipulate settings that specify whether web sites can use features such as cookies, JavaScript, and plug-ins	contentSettings	Allows an extension to change settings that control whether web sites can use features such as cookies, JavaScript, and plug-ins. Content settings allows extensions to customize Chrome's behavior on a per-site basis instead of globally. Required if the extension uses the chrome.contentSettings module.
✓	None	contextMenus	Allows an extension to add items to Chrome's context menus. Required if the extension uses the chrome.contextMenus module.
✓	None	cookies	Allows an extension to retrieve, modify, and remove cookies. Required if the extension uses the chrome.cookies module.
?	Page debugger backend	debugger	Allows remote debugging of a Chrome tab. Required if using the experimental debugger module.

---

[18] Google Chrome Extensions Permission Warnings. http://developer.chrome.com/extensions/permissions_warnings.html

Risk	Warning Message	Permission	Description
✓	None	experimental	Allows an extension to use experimental Chrome extension APIs. Required if the extension uses any chrome.experimental.* APIs. If you install an extension with this permission it will be blocked by default and this message will display: "*Loading extensions with 'experimental' is turned off by default. You can enable 'Experimental Extensions APIs' by visiting chrome://flags.*"
✓	None	extension	Allows an extension to send messages to other pages within an extension. Frequently used by Content Scripts in an extension.
◔	Detect your physical location	geolocation	Allows an extension to use the proposed HTML5 geolocation API without prompting the user for permission.
◔	Read and modify your browsing history	history	Allows an extension to add, remove, and query the browser's record of visited pages. Required if the extension uses the chrome.history module.
✓	None	idle	Allows an extension to sleep for a certain amount of time and then call a callback function. Required if the extension uses the chrome.idle module.
✓	None	keybinding	Allows an extension to register keyboard shortcuts to trigger specific actions in the extension.
◔	Manage your apps, extensions, and themes	management	Allows management of installed apps and extensions. Required if the extension uses the chrome.management module.
✓	None	notifications	Allows the extension to use the proposed HTML5 notification API without calling permission methods.
?	Access the content of the pages you visit	pageCapture	Allows saving a tab content in the RFC standard MHTML format.
?	Manipulate privacy-related settings	privacy	Allows an extension to control usage of the features in Chrome that can affect a user's privacy. Required if the extension uses the chrome.privacy module.
⬤	Access your data on all web sites	proxy	Allows an extension to manage Chrome's proxy settings. Required if the extension uses the chrome.proxy module.
✓	None	storage	Allows storage, retrieval, and tracking of changes to user data. Required if the extension uses the chrome.storage module.

Risk	Warning Message	Permission	Description
	Access your tabs and browsing activity	tabs	Allows an extension to create, modify, remove, and rearrange tabs with the browser's tab system. Required if the extension uses the chrome.tabs or chrome.windows module.
	Read and modify your browsing history	topSites	Allows access to the top sites that are displayed on the new tab page. Required if the extensions uses the chrome.topSites module.
✓	None	tts	Plays synthesized text to speech from an extension of app. Required if the extension uses the chrome.tts module.
?	Access all text spoken using synthesized speech	ttsEngine	Allows implementing a text to speech engine from an extension. Required if the extension uses the chrome.ttsEngine module.
✓	None	unlimitedStorage	Provides an unlimited quota for storing HTML5 client-side data, such as databases and local storage files.
	Access your tabs and browsing activity	webNavigation	Allows receiving of notifications about the status of navigation requests of the UI. Required if the extension uses the chrome.webNavigation module.
✓	None	webRequest	Allows an extension to intercept, block, and modify web requests and to observe and analyze web traffic in an asynchronous manner. Required if the extension uses the chrome.webRequest module.
✓	None	webRequestBlocking	Same as webRequest but in a synchronous manner.
	Access your tabs and browsing activity	windows	Same as the tabs permission.
	Warning message varies based on its use as does the risk. Usually low or medium risk is involved.	*URL pattern*	A URL pattern is used to describe access to a particular web site. When used by itself, it can mean an extension can access all data on a web site. When used with other permissions, it can mean the particular functionality the permission represents can access the data on a web site. Required if the extension wants to interact with the code running on certain web pages. Also known as a host permission.
⚠	Access all data on your computer and the web sites you visit	plugins entry	This is a separate field in the manifest file, rather than a permission, which declares the extension uses an NPAPI plugin.

Table 15: Chrome warning messages and their corresponding permission entry

5.4 Appendix D: PowerShell Scripts

The PowerShell scripts in this appendix assume an internet connection and will retrieve the latest version number for Chrome from **http://omahaproxy.appspot.com/win**. The scripts needs to run with administrative privileges and workstations must be able to accept and respond to WMI queries for the script to retrieve the currently installed Chrome version number. The scripts assume Chrome has been installed in the default location.

The script below will only check one computer at a time so it may run for several hours on a large domain. PowerShell version 1 or above is required on the machine used to run the script.

```
# Get the Current Version of Chrome from the internet. http://omahaproxy.appspot.com/win
$wc = new-object system.net.WebClient
$wc.proxy = $proxy
Try {
    $webpage = $wc.DownloadData("http://omahaproxy.appspot.com/win")
    $global:applicationVersion = [System.Text.Encoding]::ASCII.GetString($webpage)
}
Catch [system.exception] {
    "unable to contact http://omahaproxy.appspot.com/win"
    break
}

# Get all Computers from Active Directory
$computerList = @()
$strCategory = "computer"
$objDomain = New-Object System.DirectoryServices.DirectoryEntry
$objSearcher = New-Object System.DirectoryServices.DirectorySearcher
$objSearcher.SearchRoot = $objDomain
$objSearcher.Filter = ("(objectCategory=$strCategory)")
$colResults = $objSearcher.FindAll()
foreach ($objResult in $colResults){
    $objComputer = $objResult.Properties; $computerList += $objComputer.name
}

# For Each computer run a WMI query to get the installed Chrome version
# and check against current stable released version to find outdated computers
$unableToContactOrNotInstalled = @()
$upToDateComputers = @()
$outOfDateComputers = @()

foreach ($computer in $computerList)
{
    $path = "'\\Program Files\\Google\\Chrome\\Application\\'"
    if ((Get-WmiObject -Class Win32_OperatingSystem -ComputerName $computer -ea 0).OSArchitecture -eq '64-bit') {
        $path = "'\\Program Files (x86)\\Google\\Chrome\\Application\\'"
    }

        $computerAppVersion = Get-WmiObject -ErrorAction silentlycontinue -ComputerName $computer -Query "SELECT * FROM CIM_DataFile WHERE
Drive = 'C:' AND Path = $path AND FileName = 'chrome' AND Extension = 'exe'" | select Version
        if("$computerAppVersion".Contains("$applicationVersion")){
                $upToDateComputers += $computer
        }
        elseif("$computerAppVersion" -eq ""){
                $unableToContactOrNotInstalled += $computer
        }
        else{
                $outOfDateComputers += $computer
        }
}

# Display a list of computers with out of date Chrome versions
if ($outOfDateComputers) {
    "`nComputers with outdated Chrome version:"
    $outOfDateComputers
} else {
    "`nNo out of date Chrome Versions found, but " + $unableToContactOrNotInstalled.Count + " computers could not be contacted or do not have
Chrome installed."
    "" + $upToDateComputers.Count + " Computers have Chrome version " + $applicationVersion + " installed, and are up to date"
}
```

The next script can check more than one computer at a time so it may complete a domain scan much faster than the previous script. PowerShell version 2 or above is required on the system used to run the script.

```
# Number of Computers to Scan in Parallel
$parallel_jobs = 40

# Get the Current Version of Chrome from the internet. http://omahaproxy.appspot.com/win
$wc = new-object system.net.WebClient
$wc.proxy = $proxy
Try {
        $webpage = $wc.DownloadData("http://omahaproxy.appspot.com/win")
        $global:UpToDateVersion = [System.Text.Encoding]::ASCII.GetString($webpage)
}
Catch [system.exception] {
        "unable to contact http://omahaproxy.appspot.com/win"
        break
}

# Get a List of all Computers from Active Directory
$computerList = @()
$strCategory = "computer"
$objDomain = New-Object System.DirectoryServices.DirectoryEntry
$objSearcher = New-Object System.DirectoryServices.DirectorySearcher
$objSearcher.SearchRoot = $objDomain
$objSearcher.Filter = ("(objectCategory=$strCategory)")
$colResults = $objSearcher.FindAll()
foreach ($objResult in $colResults){
            $objComputer = $objResult.Properties; $computerList += $objComputer.name
}

# WMI commands to run on each host computer
$script_block = {
    param($computer)

    $path = "'\\Program Files\\Google\\Chrome\\Application\\'"
    if ((Get-WmiObject -Class Win32_OperatingSystem -ComputerName $computer -ea 0).OSArchitecture -eq '64-bit') {
        $path = "'\\Program Files (x86)\\Google\\Chrome\\Application\\'"
    }

    Get-WmiObject -ErrorAction silentlycontinue -ComputerName $computer -Query "SELECT * FROM CIM_DataFile WHERE Drive = 'C:' AND Path =
$path AND FileName = 'chrome'  AND Extension = 'exe'" | select Version
}

Remove-Job *

# Start initial jobs
$task_count = $parallel_jobs
if($task_count -gt $computerList.Length) {
    $task_count = $computerList.Length
}
foreach($i in 1..$task_count) {
    $JobName = "job_$i"
    Start-Job -ScriptBlock $script_block -Name $JobName -ArgumentList $computerList[$i-1]
}

# Poll for job completion and start more jobs
$next_index = $task_count + 1
$jobCounter = 1
while($next_index -lt $computerList.Length)
{
    for( ; $jobCounter -le $computerList.Length; )
    {
        $state = [string](Get-Job "job_$jobCounter").state
        if($state -eq "Completed")
        {
            $JobName = "job_$next_index"
            Start-Job -ScriptBlock $script_block -Name $JobName -ArgumentList $computerList[$next_index-1], $path
            $next_index++
            $jobCounter++
        }
        #if all the task in the task queue is complete, then jump out
        if($next_index -ge $computerList.Length) {
            break
        }
    }
}

# Wait untill all the background task complete
get-job | wait-job

$global:unableToContact = @()
$global:upToDateComputers = @()
$global:outOfDateComputers = @()
$counter = 1
while($counter -lt $computerList.Length)
{
    $computerAppVersion = Receive-Job "job_$counter"
    if("$computerAppVersion".Contains("$global:UpToDateVersion")){
        $global:upToDateComputers += $computerList[$counter]
    }
    elseif("$computerAppVersion" -eq ""){
            $global:unableToContact += $computerList[$counter]
    }
    else{
        $global:outOfDateComputers += $computerList[$counter]
```

```
    }
    $counter++
}

# Display a list of computers with out of date Chrome versions
if ($global:outOfDateComputers) {
    "`nComputers with outdated Chrome version:"
    $global:outOfDateComputers
} else {
    "`nNo out of date Chrome Versions found, but " + $global:unableToContact.Count + " computers could not be contacted or do not have Chrome
installed."

    "" + $global:upToDateComputers.Count + " Computers have Chrome version " + $global:UpToDateVersion + " installed, and are up to date"
}
```

www.ingramcontent.com/pod-product-compliance
Lightning Source LLC
Chambersburg PA
CBHW080637290526
45790CB00007B/3104